A CLASSROOM

(and ot~~her~~ ~~poems~~)

VAL HARRIS
Illustrations by Anna Matthews

A CLASSROOM OF STARS
(and other poems)

Author & text copyright © Val Harris 2022
Illustrator copyright © Anna Matthews 2022

The right of Val Harris to be identified as the author, and Anna Matthews as the illustrator, of this book, has been asserted by them in accordance with the Copyright, Designs and Patents Act 1988.

All rights reserved by Val Harris.

No part of this publication may be reproduced or transmitted in any form by any means, electronic or mechanical, including photocopying, reading, or any information storage and retrieval system, without permission in writing from the publisher, Val Harris.

ISBN: 978-1-3999-2141-1

Published by Val Harris
at **The Little Gull Press**
www.valharris.co.uk

Book layout design by **NB Design Studio Limited**
www.nathanbest.co.uk

Printed in England

A CIP catalogue record for this book is available from the British Library.

CONTENTS

FOOD FOR THOUGHT

The World in my Chair	12
Our Round Table	13
The Dangers of Doing Handstands and Cartwheels	14
World Book Day	15
Bookworms	16
My Dad – Eco Man!	17
Food for Thought	18
My Nose	19
Staycation	20
Smells I Don't Like	21
Bling	22
Water	23
Old Things or New?	24
Water Down the Plughole	25
Where Poems Begin	26
A Lesson in Fireworks	28
Good Luck Signs	29
As – You Like it	30
Don't Be a Seagull	31
Playground Games	32
Cumulus Clouds	33

BEING YOU!

My Noisy Body	36
A Wobbly Success Story (for Luci)	37
Camping Song	38
Between My Toes	39
My Positive Pants	40
My Nan and Tea	41
What Are You Going to Do?	42
Going to Sheep	43
A Classroom of Stars	45
Goal!	46
Being You	47
Smelly Feet	48
Feeling a Bit Uppity	49
Thank you to my Teacher	50
Things I Must Remember not to Do	51

TO BEE
(Poems about insects, animals and other creatures)

Frogs	54
What is an Earwig?	55
Bella Rules	56
My Dog, the Critic	58
To Bee	59
Can I have a Frog Please?	60
What the Horses See at Night	61
Cow Pat Splats!	62
Earth Worm Facts	63
Some Dinosaur Superlatives	64
Twitter Feed	66
Cuckoo!	67
Spiders	68
I'm an Armadillidiidae (and my name, it rhymes with tidy)	69
Beast from the East	70
The Greedy Fox	71

A BIT OF NONSENSE

Musical Discord	74
A Bit of Nonsense	75
A Smelly Rhyme (Limerick 1)	76
A Hairy Tale (Limerick 2)	77
A Llama-land (Limerick 3)	78
Owls Without Vowels	79
Wristicles and Blisticles	80
Word Play	81
An Idioms Tale	82
Wonky	83
Who Am I?	84
Bonkers	85

DEDICATIONS TO:

Charles David Schueler, my Dad, who inspired in me a lifelong love of children's and adult poetry from the books and poems of Robert Louis Stevenson, Lewis Carroll, Edward Lear, Hilaire Belloc, Christina Rossetti, Elizabeth Barrett Browning, W H Auden, Louis MacNiece, Spike Milligan, to name but a few! And who encouraged me to read, read, and write my own stories and poems. Thanks Dad!

Luci, Sophia, Isla, Elijah, Lucas, Remy, Milo
(my own Classroom of Stars)

CREATE YOUR OWN POEM

FOOD FOR THOUGHT

THE WORLD IN MY CHAIR

Whenever I can
I curl up in my chair
Then the magic begins,
I can go anywhere.

I don't need a ticket
a train or a car.
My journey is different
so near, yet so far.

All that I need
is a book in my hands,
and a story to read
about make believe lands.

The author will take me
wherever they go.
Through pages and chapters,
the magic will grow.

I might be a tiger
afloat in a boat.
Or a knight, from a castle,
crossing a moat.

I could be an agent
solving big crimes.
Or a king or a queen
from far away times.

A pirate in Neverland,
sailing an ocean.
A mermaid in charge
of an ocean's commotion.

A spaceman floating
around on the moon.
Someone who flies
in a great big balloon.

I can go anywhere,
I can be anyone.
That's why reading books
is SO MUCH FUN!

OUR ROUND TABLE

Our table has no corners,
there's no one at the end.
No-one in the middle
and no-one round the bend.

No-one is the head of it
and no-one gets left out.
We see and hear each other
So, no-one has to shout!

Everyone is equal
and everyone can see,
all the other members
of our round family.

THE DANGERS OF DOING HANDSTANDS AND CARTWHEELS

I tried to do a handstand but
the blood rushed to my head.
I kept collapsing on the floor
so, I did a cartwheel instead.

I rolled and rolled and rolled along
just like Vitruvian man,
the one Leonardo da Vinci drew;
just catch me if you can!

Head over heels and hand over hand
across the living room floor.
Rolling, whirling, round and round
until I hit the door!

WORLD BOOK DAY

Who shall I go as?
What will I be?
Maybe a Tiger
Who's hungry for tea?

Harry Potter, Hermione,
The Cat in the Hat?
A Snail, or a Whale
Or Ratine the rat?

Stickman, a Gruffalo,
The Witch from the West?
A Wild Thing, a Pirate,
Oh, what will be best?

Maybe Jane Austen,
Will Shakespeare would do.
Michael Morpurgo
Or Winnie the Pooh?

Peter Rabbit, or Alice,
Toy Story – which toy?
Woody, Buzz Lightyear?
Perhaps Billionaire Boy?

Who shall I go as,
Please help me decide.
I just cannot choose
The book lover cried.

The decision is driving me
Right round the bend!
By the time I've decided
World Book Day will end!

BOOKWORMS

Bookworms are seen in all shapes and sizes
And some call a bookworm a 'swot'.

This bookworm is hungry for paper and story,
To nibble at chapters, and chew on a plot.

This ravenous bookworm is munching on words
And I slowly devour the lot!

MY DAD - ECO MAN!

It all goes in the re-cycling bin
cardboard, papers, bottles, tin.
Mum puts it in, dad takes it out.
It might be useful, we hear him shout.

My dad up-cycled a cardboard box
for a fledgling that fell from its nest.
He turned it into a cosy bed
and the baby was rather impressed.

He shredded the paper to line the box,
a bottle he used for a feeder.
My dad's a brilliant inventor,
an Eco up-cycling leader!

FOOD FOR THOUGHT

Liver and bacon?
You must be mistaken
I'd never eat something
As yucky as that!

Onions and tripe,
A lemon, unripe?
I think I would rather
Eat my hat!

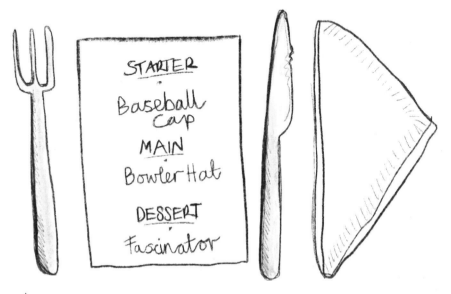

MY NOSE

My nose has no legs but it runs.
It's fixed but it grows if I lie.
It flares when it's mad
Or something smells bad
And it blows whenever I cry!

STAYCATION

We're going to go on safari,
Mum and Dad decided.
Oh yes, yes let's, all of us cried
But then the excitement subsided.

Will the lions come into our tent?
Will the elephants trample it down?
Will snakes and spiders scare us at night?
I'm not sure, Dad said, with a frown.

Will the monkeys steal our pants?
Will the sun burn our heads bright red?
Will a leopard drag all of us up in a tree?
Right, cried Dad, enough said.

I think we'll just go to the seaside,
We can swim and fish from the pier.
We can eat fish and chips out of paper,
And I can enjoy a cold beer.

What if the weather is windy?
What if we're swept, out to sea?
By a tidal wave, forty feet high.
What? Dad groaned, goodness me.

Is there nowhere safe to go?
There seems to be nowhere at all.
I'll put up a tent in the garden,
And leave our bags in the hall.

SMELLS I DON'T LIKE

Cabbage water down the sink.
Rubbish bins that really stink.

Smelly fish and stinky meat.
Rotten eggs and cheesy feet.

Brussels sprouts and school canteens.
My sister when she's eaten beans!

Pickled onions in a jar.
Petrol fumes inside the car.

Dog poo squelching on my shoe,
Smells so bad and sticks like glue.

Smells I don't like; smells I do:
Peppermint, peaches, how about you?

BLING

There's a girl at school, a flashy thing,
Whose arms are always full of bling.
I don't know how she lugs it round,
It must all weigh a hundred pounds!
If bling could sing, she'd blow the roof,
Our ears would ring, we'd have the proof,
That wearing so much flashy bling
Can be a very dangerous thing!

WATER

What would we do without water?
How would our teeth get clean?
How would we boil a kettle
Or use a washing machine?

How would we wash our faces,
How would we flush the loo?
Without a tap full of water,
What do you think we would do?

OLD THINGS OR NEW?

What do you like,
old things or new?
The ramparts of castles,
or a skyscraper view?

The cloud piercing Shard?
Cleopatra's needle?
The odd looking, Gherkin,
or St. Paul's Cathedral?

A house full of beams
and old cobbled lanes?
Or a big modern flat
in a city of cranes?

I rather like both,
it depends how I feel.
I like going round on
the Millennium Wheel,

Then my eye can enjoy
a breath-taking view
of old things, amongst
a great skyline of new.

WATER DOWN THE PLUGHOLE
(A poem about the Coriolis effect on bathwater
- North or South? Fact or myth?)

Filling a bath
Is a jolly good laugh
Until someone pulls the plug!
Then off it goes
In a clockwise flow,
Down the drain with a glug!

Unless you live
On the opposite side,
Then down the drain it goes,
Round and round
The opposite way
In an anti-clockwise flow.

WHERE POEMS BEGIN

They begin with a thought in the morning,
when I wake up from dreaming, in bed.
They dance on the wall,
they're a voice in the hall,
and they wander around in my head.

They begin with the sun in the garden,
or a walk on a sharp winter's day.
With a crunch in the snow,
a red sunset glow;
the stars in the Milky Way.

Or a gleam from the moon on a rooftop.
The sounds of a city awake.
The buzz of a bee,
the crash of the sea,
and reflections that gleam on a lake.

A face staring out of a window,
a sentence I read in a book.
A movie I've seen,
or a place that I've been,
there's a poem wherever I look.

Poems begin anywhere, anytime,
they pop up wherever I go.
They enter my head,
where they wait to be fed
and they grow, and they grow and they grow!

A LESSON IN FIREWORKS
(metaphorically speaking)

When I was sent home from school
Mum said: there's going to be fireworks.

Fireworks, I thought? Fireworks?
Am I going to be punished with fireworks?

It didn't make sense, until mum and dad
Both came whizzing up the stairs,

Rockets flying out of their ears and nose,
Their eyes spinning like Catherine Wheels,

And the words they spoke were **BANGERS!**
Now I know what a fireworks metaphor is!

GOOD LUCK SIGNS!

We've got bats up in the attic,
One landed on my bed.
I put my clothes on backwards,
And a bird pooed on my head.

My ears are feeling itchy,
We live at number eight.
We've adopted a gorilla
And there's ivy round our gate!

As - You Like It

As brave as a lion
As strong as an ox
As wise as an owl
As sly as a fox

As hard as nails
As soft as silk
As warm as toast
As cool as milk

As fresh as a daisy
As old as time
As sweet as honey
As sour as a lime

As steadfast as rock
As changeable as weather
As soft as goose down
As tough as old leather

DON'T BE A SEAGULL

Stalkers and stealers,
Muggers, marauders.
Squabbling snatchers,
Loud mouthed squawkers.

Bullies and braggers,
Raucous shriekers.
Sneaky scavengers,
Mischief seekers.

(PS - not all seagulls are bad - said a seagull!)

PLAYGROUND GAMES

Who swung the rope for skipping?
Who threw the hopscotch stone?
Me and all the rest of us
While you stood on your own.

You didn't join in games with us
We never wondered why?
Me and all the rest of us
Didn't think you might be shy.

So, if there's someone standing by
With nothing much to say,
Maybe all of us could ask
If they would like to play!

Cumulus Clouds

I watched them arriving
This morning, this morning.
I saw them there
On the edge of the day.

Like smoke on the water,
Greedily, greedily,
Swallowing sky
And slurring their words.

I felt them drift over me,
Softly, so softly,
Devouring me totally
Out of this world.

CREATE YOUR OWN POEM

BEING YOU!

MY NOISY BODY

My tummy growls when I'm hungry,
My heart has a beat like a drum.
My teeth have a habit of chattering,
And my ears sometimes ring or hum.

My bottom goes 'pop!' without warning.
My bones often make a loud crack!
My fingernails tap on the table top,
And my lips like to smack, when I snack.

A WOBBLY SUCCESS STORY
(for Luci)

Dad says: *this is how you do it,*
just push, pedal, gli-i-ide.
But it's not that easy
learning to ride

a two wheeled wobbly monster,
with a mind of its own.
Push, pedal, wobble, wobble,
crash down on the stone.

Come on, Dad says, *try again,*
just believe you can.
I'm trying Dad, but falling off
wasn't in my plan!

Hold on to me Dad, Da-a-ad,
please don't let me go!
Okay, I'm holding the saddle,
Now push, pedal, GO!

I can't do it, I can't do it,
DA-A-AD where are you...?
Oh, look at me, I'm doing it,
I'm riding my bike – WAHOO!

CAMPING SONG

We love camping
Even in the rain.
It's raining, it's pouring,
It's bucketing again!

It's leaking through the canvas,
It's creeping round our toes.
It's got inside my sleeping bag
And now it's in my nose.

It's raining, it's pouring
But we don't care,
'cos we love camping
In the open air.

Sun's out, sun's out
Now we'll have some fun.
Camping, camping,
Fun for everyone.

We like it when it's night time,
Underneath the stars,
All around the campfire
Looking out for Mars!

We love camping
Even in the rain.
It's raining, it's pouring,
It's bucketing again!

BETWEEN MY TOES

When I go down beside the sea
I like the sand between my toes,
The curling water rushing in
As it slowly ebbs and flows.

I hear the seagull's epic shriek
And watch it glide above the sea.
I chase the little racing crabs,
Across the sand, away from me.

MY POSITIVE PANTS

If I'm feeling a little bit wobbly,
Anxious, nervous or shy,
I put on a pair of positive pants
And look the world in the eye.

In my positive pants I'm a warrior,
A leader, a queen, a king.
When I put on a pair of positive pants,
My heart begins to sing!

It doesn't matter what colour,
It doesn't matter what style,
Positive pants are for anyone
So, go on, give them a try.

Positive pants mean business,
They make me feel brave and strong.
When I'm wearing a pair of positive pants
My heart wants to burst into song!

MY NAN AND TEA

When I think of my nan
I think of tea.
That's what my nan
Meant to me.
The kettle boiling,
The teacups clink,
My nan humming
At the kitchen sink.

Early mornings,
When I stayed at her flat,
I'd hear the rattling
Of tea tray chat.
Then out of the kitchen
I'd hear her coming
With tea and biscuits
And her happy humming.

Morning my darling.
She'd say, with a hug
She'd have a cup
And I'd have a mug.
A plateful of biscuits,
Our favourite, Rich Tea,
That's how I remember
My nan and me.

WHAT ARE YOU GOING TO DO?

My parents ask, when you leave school
What are you going to do?
My answer always is the same,
I haven't got a clue!

Perhaps I'll be a rally driver
Racing fancy cars.
Or a very famous astronaut
Rocketing to Mars.

Or maybe a psychiatrist,
Sorting people out.
Or an operatic singer,
Then I can scream and shout.

I could train to be a doctor,
A dentist or a vet.
My parents like the sound of this.
I've not decided yet.

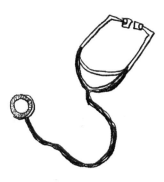

They seem to be determined
To find a path for me,
But when I dare to tell them
What I think I'd like to be -

A writer or a poet,
They both just stare at me.

But I'll publish a BESTSELLER,
Just you wait and see!

GOING TO SHEEP

If you can't sleep
Mum said, *count sheep.*
I looked all around but none were there
Not a single sheep anywhere.

SO, I COUNTED:

The leaves on the trees
Outside my room.
The flowers on the curtains,
Every bloom.

I counted the cracks
On my bedroom wall.
But I still couldn't find
Any sheep, at all.

I looked on the ceiling,
I looked on the floor.
I waited for sheep
To come through the door.

I waited and waited
But still no sheep.
I was feeling quite tired
And I fell asleep!

A CLASSROOM OF STARS

When Jake put up his hand
To answer a question
Everyone was amazed.
Jake never did that, never!
Then Saida did the same.
Saida? The quiet girl?
We were properly stunned
By these stars in our classroom
That were suddenly shining.

One by one our hands went up.
We shone and shimmered
In our classroom universe.
Brian Cox hadn't seen these stars yet.
It was our teacher who discovered them,
Finding the light that he knew
Lay inside all of us
In our classroom universe,
In his classroom of stars.

GOAL

The ball's in my lap
That I try not to drop
As my wheels whizz and spin
And I turn like a top.
We're going to win,
I can hear the crowd roar,
Urging me faster
Over the floor.
Oh, how good it feels
To be part of this band.
I race on my wheels
Then the ball's in my hand.
I aim for the net
I throw and let go.
Up goes the ball,
It's in, we win,
It's a brilliant

GOAL!

BEING YOU

Be anything you want to be,
In everything you do.
Show the world just who you are
By just being you.

Wear a silly jumper,
Wear a crazy hat.
Move like you're loving it,
Purr like a cat!

Dye your hair bright red,
Yellow, green or blue.
Be anything you want to be
By just being you!

Put your love, your heart and soul
In everything you do.
Show the world just who you are
By just being YOU!

SMELLY FEET

When I took off my shoes in the kitchen,
The dog passed out with the smell.
The cat ran out of the house with a howl
And the mice and the spiders as well.

The birds in the trees went silent,
The hens stopped laying their eggs.
And mum and the rest of the family,
Closed up their noses with pegs.

They say that my feet are smelly,
And my sister says that they reek.
But I can't smell a thing any more
Since I had Covid last week!

FEELING A BIT UPPITY

I don't want to clean up my bedroom
I don't like washing up.
I don't want to go to school today,
I just don't want to get up!

I don't want to sit and do lessons,
I don't want to get up to play,
I just want to look at my X-box
And not have to get up all day!

I don't want to get up to wash,
I'd rather be smelly instead.
I don't want to get up for dinner,
I'd rather eat biscuits in bed.

Then mum yells up the staircase:
I think you've forgotten today
Is your birthday, and if you don't get up,
Shall I chuck all your presents away?

THANK YOU TO MY TEACHER

Thank you for your inspiration,
Smiling strength and dedication.
Through the lockdowns, you were there
Helping, guiding us, with care.

The zooming maze you got us through,
The goals and work you helped with too.
The smiles you gave, the smiles you made,
Those memories will never fade.

You really made a difference
And now we'd like to share,
How grateful all of us have been
That you were teaching there.

Thank you for your kindness,
For all the lovely things you've done.
We'd like to say, from all of us,
You're teacher, number one!

THINGS I MUST REMEMBER NOT TO DO

Walk, don't run.
Talk, don't shout.
Don't put my elbows
On the table.
Don't speak
With my mouth full.
Stop fidgeting.
Don't slouch.
Don't drag my feet.

Mum, please can I...?
Don't interrupt.
But...
Don't be rude!

CREATE YOUR OWN POEM

TO BEE

(Poems about insects, animals & other creatures)

FROGS

Frogs make funny croaking sounds
They have big bulging eyes.
They're sometimes smooth and slimy;
Their tongues are long and sticky
To catch delicious flies.

WHAT IS AN EARWIG?

Nan told me, there's an Old Wives Tale
that earwigs lived in ears,
and so, the kids in olden days
were full of night time fears.

Parents used to warn them
before they went to sleep:
keep your ears well covered
where the earwigs like to creep!

They'll get into your ear canal
and stay and live at large,
sailing round your brainwaves
on a little earwig barge.

The earwig got its name, she'd say,
and give a little giggle,
because their pincers look like ears.
The wig is short for wiggle.

My mum would say, don't listen
to the stories Nan tells you.
So, I googled that Old Wives Tale,
and I think it might be true!

BELLA RULES

I'm Bella the cat with my very sleek fur,
It's shiny and black, and soft like my purr.

I live in a house with a family of four
With my very own bed and my very own door.

I chill out all day in a comfortable chair,
Curled up and wonderfully cosy in there.

The chair was reserved for dear Aunty Sue
But I named it and claimed it, as cats often do.

I purr and look cute and no-one says shoo,
From the chair they reserved for dear Aunty Sue.

I don't ask too much of the family I rule,
It's not very different from going to school.

Remember this rule: I'm not yours, you are mine,
And if you know your place, we'll get along fine.

I don't hear commands, I give them you see,
So never, no never be late with my tea.

Remember my claws can make your ears ring
As I slowly scratch down on your favourite thing!

At night when you sleep, I go out on the prowl
To meet other cats, for a neighbourhood howl.

We hunt out the creatures, tasty and nice,
We're particularly fond of fat juicy mice.

I thought you'd be grateful for something like that;
When you scream you sound like a really weird cat!

Don't think that it's better to keep me shut in.
I'll hiss and I'll howl with a terrible din.

I'm Bella the cat and we'll get along fine
If you never forget: 'I'm not yours - you are mine.'

MY DOG THE CRITIC

My dog is a very good listener,
But I think I must drive him quite mad.
I read out my poems and ask him to show
If the poem is good, or it's bad.

He lifts up an eyebrow and stares,
So, I carry on reading some more.
Until with a sigh and a look in his eye
He asks me to stop, with his paw.

TO BEE

I'd like to be a butterfly with wings as light as silk.
Or maybe just a kitten with a bowl of frothy milk

A sparkly little dragonfly zipping through the reeds.
Possibly a slimy worm wiggling through the weeds.

A stealthy growling tiger prowling through the trees,
Or just a singing skylark hanging in the breeze.

But I'm a very busy bee, living in a hive
With lots of other busy bees, working nine to five!

CAN I HAVE A FROG PLEASE?

I'm not allowed a rabbit,
I'm not allowed a dog,
It's no to an aquarium
But, can I have a frog?

If I cannot have a hamster,
A lizard or a mouse,
Please mum, can I have a frog
That lives outside the house?

A frog that needs no feeding
Or walking like a dog.
No bed to clean, or poo to pick,
Please can I have a frog?

I suppose, mum sighs, a frog
Is rather better than a dog.
(But I haven't told the whole truth
About where I'll keep that frog.)

She thinks I'll keep it outside
Underneath the shed.
But I'll sneak it in at teatime
And leave it on my bed.

WHAT THE HORSES SEE AT NIGHT

Have you ever wondered
what the horses see at night,
When all of us are sleeping
and the moon is shining bright?

Do you think they notice rabbits,
or a fox out on the prowl?
Do they look up when they hear
the high-pitched screeching, of an owl?

Do you think they see a badger,
running through the lanes?
Or see the bright lights in the sky
from satellites and planes?

I don't think they notice very much,
except the grass they eat.
They rarely put their heads up
so, they mostly see their feet!

COW PAT SPLATS

When you see a cow pat
splattered in a field
I bet you never think about
the food that splat might yield!

Underneath the cow pat
a world of wonder lies.
Where spiders, worms and beetles
eat eggs laid by the flies.

And if that sounds revolting
and you hate the look and smell,
we fertilise our veg with dung,
and splats make bricks as well.

So, when you screw your nose up
and step across that pat,
remember that to someone
it's a very useful splat!

EARTH WORM FACTS

My teacher told me things today
That may sound rather mad.
He said, worms don't have faces.
That seems a little sad.

Without any eyes, or an ear, or a nose,
How do they find their tea?
And when they wriggle through the dirt,
How does an earthworm see?

He also said that worms have not
Just one small brain, but two.
Do worms have more to think about
than either me, or you?

And when it comes to beating hearts,
The earthworm, it has five!
It takes a very tuneful beat
To keep a worm alive!

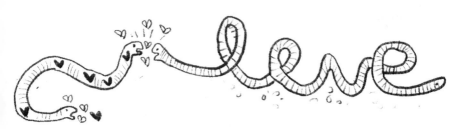

SOME DINOSAUR SUPERLATIVES

THE MIGHTIEST AND STRONGEST

Tyrannosaurus Rex,
King of the dinosaurs.
A mighty fearsome theropod,
With awesome crunching jaws.

THE SMARTEST

The Troodon's brain was supersized,
And some say it was smart.
I wonder if the Troodon
Could do algebra or art?

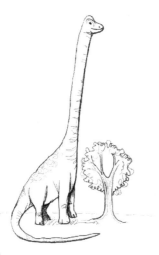

PROBABLY THE TALLEST

The mighty Ultrasaurus
Was, at least six stories high.
You'd crick your neck to see its face
When that went clomping by.

(One of) THE FASTEST

Velociraptor was a sprinter
With a crazy looking face.
If that dinosaur was chasing you
You'd want to win the race!

(One of) THE DEADLIEST

Allosaurus was a vicious beast
With serrated teeth in its jaws.
Long strong arms to hold you tight
And sharp, curved ripping claws.

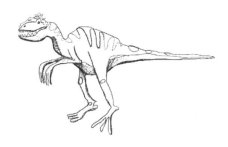

THE WHACKIEST

Ankylosaurus was an herbivore
With a spiky armoured back.
A very small brain, but a club like tail
that could give you a painful thwack!

How many dinosaur superlatives you can think of?

TWITTER FEED

There's a tweeting in the hedgerows
Snap-chatting in the air.
She's filling up the feeders,
Excitement everywhere.

The twitter feed is going mad
It's buzzing round like bees.
She's filling up the feeders
With fat balls, nuts and seeds.

Every single one is full
For every bird around;
And mealworms for the robins
To peck at, on the ground.

The messages are streaming
Across the fields and woods.
Airwave tweeting far and wide:
She's hanging out the goods!

They're tweeting in the hedgerows
Snap-chatting in the trees,
It's a twitter feed for everyone
As long as they tweet *please!*

Cuckoo!

The cuckoo doesn't understand
The trouble that it brings,
The worry for the other birds
As soon as cuckoo sings.

The lazy cuckoo lays its eggs
In any random nest,
Then baby cuckoo hatches out
A large unwelcome guest.

It keeps the host mum busy
Trying to feed the giant bird.
She soon becomes exhausted
With a job that's quite absurd.

Her search for food is endless
To feed the cuckoo's din,
Her ears are ringing like a bell,
She's looking rather thin.

At last, the cuckoo fledges,
There's silence in the nest.
The host mum sighs with great relief;
She's earned herself a rest!

SPIDERS

I wish that spiders weren't so big and hairy
I wish they didn't look so very scary.
I wish they wouldn't give me such a fright
When they run across my bedroom floor at night.

I wish they wouldn't scuttle up the wall,
I wish they didn't vanish when they fall.
I wish they wouldn't hang out in the bath
I wish they didn't make my sister laugh.

I wish that spiders didn't make me scream.
I wish they wouldn't hang out when I dream.
I wish I didn't find those spiders scary,
I suppose they're not that big, but they ARE hairy!

I'M AN ARMADILLIDIIDAE
(and my name it rhymes with tidy)

I'm an Armadillidiidae,
Or wood louse if you please,
I have a lot of nicknames
And some are made from cheese.

In Guildford I'm a Cheesy-Bob,
In Devon a Chiggy-pig.
In Ireland I'm a Jomit
And somewhere a Cheesy-wig.

In Reading I'm a Cheese-log
In Scotland, Chucky-pigs.
Slunkers, Sows and Timpers.
In Dorset, Chiggy-wigs.

I'm scared of creepy spiders
They think I'm nice to eat,
That's why you might find a pile of me
Lying at your feet!

I'm an Armadillidiidae,
Just say it as you please.
Perhaps the spiders like me
Because I taste of cheese.

BEAST FROM THE EAST

There's a beast from the east
outside, on the prowl,
and it yells all night
with a roar and a howl.

A beast from the east
with mighty claws,
that scrabble and scratch
at the windows and doors.

A beast in the trees,
and the branches quake,
and it batters the roof
with a rattle and shake.

I think it's living
in the garden shed.
It's the wind, Mum says,
but it's a LION in my head.

THE GREEDY FOX

Slinky, sly and russet red
The greedy fox comes creeping,
Sneaking round my chicken run
When all of us are sleeping.

I know she has to feed her cubs,
But not with my sweet hen.
Hurry by please, Mrs. Fox,
And find another pen!

CREATE YOUR OWN POEM

A BIT OF NONSENSE

'Nonsense is taking an absurdity to the point where the reader laughs but doesn't know why. It's about wreaking havoc with the English language and trying to puzzle the reader as much as you can.'
(Spike Milligan)

MUSICAL DISCORD

Three music girls live in an orchestra pit:
Harp, Viola and Cello.
They spend all day singing and playing,
And messing about with a fellow!

Harp's in love with a violin,
And Cello fancies the flute.
Viola is drawn to the harpsichord
But she's also in love with the lute.

The music they play is chaotic,
Nothing they play is in tune.
The Conductor threw down his baton,
And danced with the big bassoon.

A BIT OF NONSENSE

Nine kids lived in a tumbled-down farm
Their mother was a goat.
They shared the place with fifty drums
But none could play a note.

Now in those drums were baby kits
But none of these were cats.
There also were a group of pups,
But these were baby rats.

If kits aren't cats, and pups are rats
And kids don't speak, they bleat.
What a strange collection
For anyone to meet.

A SMELLY RHYME
(Limerick 1)

There was a young lady from Spain,
Who tripped up and fell down a drain,
The lady cried: ooh-er!
As she swept down the sewer,
And nobody saw her again.

A HAIRY TALE
(Limerick 2)

A lady with masses of hair
Was making her way to the fair.
A monkey on stilts,
Three pigeons in kilts,
Got a ride in her hair, with no fare.

A LLAMA-LAND
(Limerick 3)

A boy near of field full of Llamas,
Sleepwalked in that field in pyjamas.
The rumour, it seemed,
Was he screamed as he dreamed,
And frightened the Llamas and farmers.

🦉WLS W-TH🦉-T V🦉W-LS

Th-s -s - p🦉-m
W-th🦉-t -ny v🦉w-ls
C-n y🦉- g--ss
Wh-t -t s-ys?

-nd

👁

l🦉v-

🦉 🦉 🦉

WRISTICLES AND BLISTICLES

I had a great big blisticle
Upon my bony wristicle.
Mum said, you need a plasticle,
To cover up the blisticle,
That looks a little ghasticle,
Upon your bony wristicle.

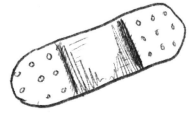

WORD PLAY

A lazy cat
Lay on a mat
And closed its lazy eyes.

A crazy bat
Flew at the cat
And shouted out: surprise!

Get off the mat
You lazy cat,
The crazy bat cried out.

The lazy cat
Stared at the bat
And said: no need to shout.

Cats like to nap,
Bats like to flap,
But the two don't go together.

Come rain or shine,
Come snow or fine,
Not in any kind of weather.

The crazy bat
Said: fancy that,
And doubled up with laughter.

It said: goodbye,
Then flew up high
And hung out on a rafter.

An Idioms Tale

Because of a storm in a teacup,
We missed the boat.
Time and tide wait for no-one.
It was the straw that broke the camel's back.
But mum said, all good things come to those who wait.
I thought she was beating around the bush
And I was a bit bent out of shape about it.
But I decided to let her off the hook,
And I got rid of the chip on my shoulder.
If that ship had sailed, then somewhere,
Between the devil and the deep blue sea,
another ship will come in.
And in the meantime
We'll make hay while the sun shines!

WONKY

I hung my picture on the wall
But it tilted to one side.
I couldn't get that picture straight
No matter how I tried.

My picture was a beauty,
A seascape with a cliff,
But it's hanging at an angle
And the view is all skew-whiff!

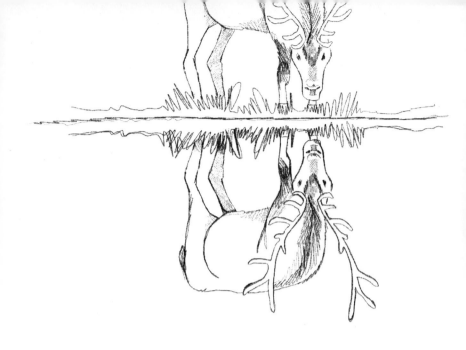

WHO AM I?

I went to the pond and what did I see?
Two little Moorhens staring at me.
Why are you staring? and the Moorhens said,
There are two big branches sticking out of your head.

I looked in the water and what did I see?
My own reflection looking at me
With two big branches sticking out of my head.
They're not branches, they're antlers, I said.

BONKERS

Today I had a silly thought
Whilst standing on my head,
An upside down and bonkers thought
My mind was being fed.

What if clouds were soft meringues
And the sun was a big fried egg?
What if rain was lemonade
And the sky was slices of bread.

What if trees were celery sticks
And the leaves were pieces of cheese.
If the sea was made of sour cream
And the grass was mushy peas.

What if planets were maltesers
And each of the stars was a pea?
We could eat up the whole of the universe
How bonkers would that be?

We could dip the sky in the sunshine
And wash down the clouds with the rain.
Scoop the trees in the oceans
And then go round again.

Today I had a silly thought
Whilst standing on my head,
An upside down and bonkers thought -
I think I'll go to bed.

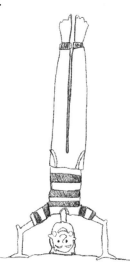

This book
Has come to an
End

Eventually a
New one will
Descend.

Author

VAL HARRIS was born in London and brought up in the wonderful countryside of Buckinghamshire. She has been writing stories and poems for a long time, but more recently has focused on poetry for children. Val has had poems for children published in The Dirigible Balloon, Paperbound Magazine, The Caterpillar Magazine and Little Thoughts Press.

She also writes poetry and stories for grown-ups, and has self-published four novels. Her website is: www.valharris.co.uk and you can find Val on:

Twitter @dragontripper (Val Poet)
Instagram: @Val Poet
Instagram: @The Little Gull Press

Illustrator

ANNA MATTHEWS is a Farnham based illustrator. She is a constant scribbler, doodler and a sketcher -always with a pen, pencil a collection of old faded papers or salvaged slate at hand. Her family of big and small people inspire her, those that sit beside her and those that now flutter by. You can find Anna on:

Instagram: @annamatthewsillustration
Facebook: @AnnaMatthewsIllustration
Etsy: @ConstantScribbler

ACKNOWLEDGEMENTS

The Dirigible Balloon (www.dirigibleballoon.org) for first publishing (2021/22) the following poems featured in this book: **Twitter Feed, Cow Pat Splats, Word Play, A Wobbly Success Story,** and **Our Round Table.**

The Caterpillar (www.thecaterpillarmagazine.com) for first publishing (2022): **Smelly Feet**